NAVESINK SCHOOL

Surprises

An I Can Read Book®

Surprises

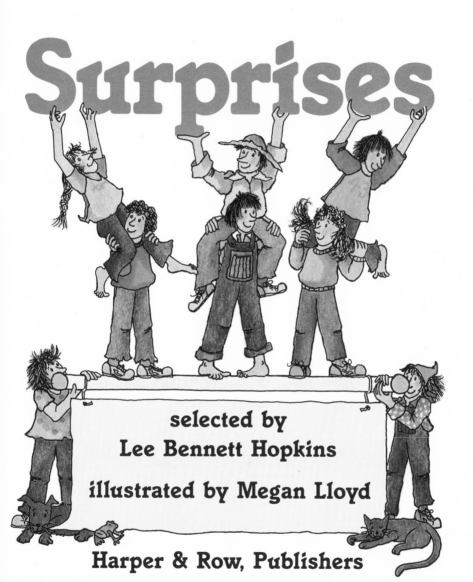

selected by
Lee Bennett Hopkins

illustrated by Megan Lloyd

Harper & Row, Publishers

Library of Congress Cataloging in Publication Data
Main entry under title:
Surprises.

(An I can read book)
"A Charlotte Zolotow book"—Half t.p.
Includes index.
Summary: A collection of short poems by Marchette
Chute, Myra Cohn Livingston, Aileen Fisher, Lee Bennett
Hopkins, and other authors.
    1. Children's poetry, American.   [1. American poetry—
Collections]   I. Hopkins, Lee Bennett.   II. Lloyd,
Megan, ill.   III. Series.
PS586.3.S87 1984   811'.54'0809282   83-47712
ISBN 0-06-022584-X
ISBN 0-06-022585-8 (lib. bdg.)

Designed by Al Cetta
2 3 4 5 6 7 8 9 10
First Edition

Acknowledgments

Every effort has been made to trace the ownership of all copyrighted material and
to secure the necessary permissions to reprint these selections. In the event of any
question arising as to the use of any material, the editor and the publisher, while
expressing regret for any inadvertent error, will be happy to make the necessary
correction in future printings. Thanks are due to the following for permission to
reprint the copyrighted materials listed below:

Atheneum Publishers, Inc. for "Never Mind the Rain" from *Hurry, Hurry, Mary
Dear! and Other Nonsense Poems.* Copyright © 1976 by N. M. Bodecker. (A
Margaret K. McElderry Book.); "Bedtime" from *8 A.M. Shadows.* Copyright
© 1965 by Patricia Hubbell; "Who to Pet and Who Not to" from *One Winter Night
in August and Other Nonsense Jingles.* Copyright © 1975 by X. J. Kennedy. (A
Margaret K. McElderry Book.) All reprinted with the permission of Atheneum
Publishers, Inc.

4

5

To William C. Morris—
A good book-friend

LBH

For Judy and Stan

ML

Who
to Pet

Plans

by Maxine W. Kumin

When I grow up, I plan to keep

Eleven cats, and let them sleep

On any bedspread that they wish,

And feed them people's tuna fish.

Who to Pet and Who Not to

by X. J. Kennedy

Go pet a kitten, pet a dog,

Go pet a worm for practice,

But don't go pet a porcupine—

You want to be a cactus?

11

Hamsters

by Marci Ridlon

Hamsters are the nicest things

That anyone could own.

I like them even better than

Some dogs that I have known.

Their fur is soft, their faces nice.

They're small when they are grown.

And they sit inside your pocket

When you are all alone.

Freckles

by Aileen Fisher

Jerry has freckles,

peppered like spice.

And Jerry has a pony

I rode on twice.

I think freckles

are *awfully* nice.

13

My Dog

by Myra Cohn Livingston

He didn't bark *at* anything—

a cat,

a bird,

a piece of string,

a siren or a silly toad,

a pick-up truck along the road,

14

a fence,

a bone,

a chewed-up shoe—

He barked because he *wanted* to.

My Kitten

by Marchette Chute

Kitten, my kitten,

Soft and dear,

I am so glad

That we are here

Sitting together

Just us two

You loving me

And me loving you.

Creep, Crawl, Fly

Caterpillars

by Aileen Fisher

What do caterpillars do?

Nothing much but chew and chew.

What do caterpillars know?

Nothing much but how to grow.

18

They just eat what by and by

will make them be a butterfly,

But that is more than I can do

however much I chew and chew.

19

Bee Song

by Carl Sandburg

Bees in the late summer sun

Drone their song

Of yellow moons

Trimming black velvet,

Droning, droning a sleepysong.

Bees

by Russell Hoban

Honeybees are very tricky—

Honey doesn't make them sticky.

21

Wasps

by Dorothy Aldis

Wasps like coffee.

Syrup.

Tea.

Coca-Cola.

Butter.

Me.

Bugs

by Karla Kuskin

I am very fond of bugs.

I kiss them

And I give them hugs.

23

Untitled

by Christina Rossetti

Hurt no living thing:

Ladybug nor butterfly,

Nor moth with dusty wing,

Nor cricket chirping cheerily,

Nor grasshopper so light of leap,

Nor dancing gnat, nor beetle fat,

Nor harmless worms that creep.

At
the Top
of
My Voice

Last Laugh

by Lee Bennett Hopkins

They all laughed when I told them
I wanted to be

A woman in space
Floating so free.

But they won't laugh at me
When they finally see
My feet up on Mars
And my face on TV.

26

At the Top of My Voice

by Felice Holman

When I stamp

The ground thunders,

When I shout

The world rings,

When I sing

The air wonders

How I do such things.

27

Keepsakes

by Leland B. Jacobs

I keep bottle caps,

I keep strings,

I keep keys and corks

And all such things.

28

When people say,

"What good are they?"

The answer's hard to get

For just how I will use them all

I don't know yet.

Ice Skating

by Sandra Liatsos

Higher and higher

I glide in the sky,

My feet flashing silver,

A star in each eye.

With wind at my back

I can float, I can soar.

The earth cannot hold me

In place anymore.

Hope

by Langston Hughes

Sometimes when I'm lonely,

Don't know why,

Keep thinkin' I won't be lonely

By and by.

31

Everybody Says

by Dorothy Aldis

Everybody says

I look just like my mother.

Everybody says

I'm the image of Aunt Bee.

Everybody says

My nose is like my father's.

But *I* want to look like ME!

Boats, Trains, and Planes

Taking Off

Anonymous

The airplane taxis down the field

And heads into the breeze.

It lifts its wheels above the ground

It skims above the trees.

It rises high and higher

Away up toward the sun,

It's just a speck against the sky

—And now it's gone!

Up in the Air

by James S. Tippett

Zooming across the sky,

Like a great bird you fly,

    Airplane

    Silvery white

    In the light.

Turning and twisting in the air,

When shall I ever be there,

    Airplane,

    Piloting you

    Far in the blue?

The Subway Train

by Leland B. Jacobs

The subway train, the

subway train,

If you'll permit me to explain,

Is like a busy beetle black

That scoots along a silver track;

And, whether it be night or day,

The beetle has to light its way,

Because the only place it's

     found

Is deep, deep, deep, deep, under-

     ground.

Out for a Ride

by Claudia Lewis

A little puff boat,

white as a marshmallow,

whiffing down the river.

  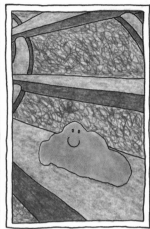

A Peanut

Anonymous

A peanut sat on the railroad track,

Its heart was all a-flutter—

Choo-choo train

Comes round the bend,

Toot toot!

Peanut butter!

I Wonder

by Charlotte Zolotow

A boat steams slowly down the river

this shiny sunny day.

I wonder who is on it

and if it's going far away.

40

I send good wishes to you,

someone just like me,

wondering who I am on shore

that you can hardly see.

41

Flying

by Eve Merriam

When you fly in a plane,

You go up past the rain.

It's odd to see the clouds below,

Looking just like banks of snow.

Over the hills of the sky you glide;

The plane is a sled for you to ride.

42

Rain, Sun, and Snow

Sudden Storm

by Elizabeth Coatsworth

The rain comes in sheets

Sweeping the streets,

Here, here, and here,

Umbrellas appear,

44

Red, blue, yellow, green,

They tilt and they lean

Like mushrooms, like flowers

That grow when it showers.

45

Never Mind the Rain

by N. M. Bodecker

Never mind the rain!
It doesn't leave a stain.

Never mind the snow!
It melts before you know.

But rain and snow together!
That's pretty nasty weather.

46

First Snow

by Marie Louise Allen

Snow makes whiteness where it falls.

The bushes look like popcorn balls.

And places where I always play,

Look like somewhere else today.

47

In August

by Marchette Chute

When the sun is strong

And the day is hot,

We move around

At a peaceful trot.

We don't wear much

In the way of clothes

And we squirt ourselves

With a garden hose.

Change in the Weather

by Ilo Orleans

I think it would be very good

To have some snow and sleet

In summer when

We need it most

To drive away the heat.

50

Sun After Rain

by Norma Farber

Rain, rain,

went away.

Sun came out

with pipe of clay,

blew a bubble

whole-world-wide,

stuck a rainbow

on one side.

51

Downpour

by Myra Cohn Livingston

Boots

and

hat

and

coat

    for rain,

    and me, *inside* the windowpane!

Good
Night

In the Night

by Marchette Chute

When I wake up and it is dark

And very far from day

I sing a humming sort of tune

To pass the time away.

I hum it loud, I hum it soft,

I hum it low and deep,

And by the time I'm out of breath

I've hummed myself to sleep.

Night Bear

by Lee Bennett Hopkins

In the dark of night

    when all is still

And I'm half-sleeping in my bed;

It's good to know

    my Teddy-bear

is snuggling at my head.

Covers

by Nikki Giovanni

Glass covers windows

    to keep the cold away

Clouds cover the sky

    to make a rainy day

Nighttime covers

    all the things that creep

Blankets cover me

    when I'm asleep

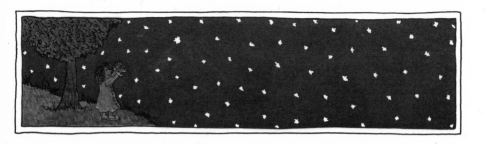

De Koven

by Gwendolyn Brooks

You are a dancy little thing,

You are a rascal, star!

You seem to be so near to me,

And yet you are so far.

If I could get you in my hands

You'd never get away.

I'd keep you with me always.

You'd shine both night and day.

Bedtime

by Patricia Hubbell

Hop away

Skip away

Jump away

Leap!

Day is all crumpled

And lies in a heap.

Jump away

Skip away

Hop away

Creep!

Night comes and coaxes

The world to sleep.

59

Sun for Breakfast

by Norma Farber

Rise up and look
at pond, at brook.

Night now is gone.
Morning upon
her silver tray
is serving day.

All you who wake
up hungry: take!

Index of Authors and Titles